POETRY now

WHEN EMOTIONS COLLIDE

Edited by

Rebecca Mee

First published in Great Britain in 2001 by
POETRY NOW
Remus House,
Coltsfoot Drive,
Peterborough, PE2 9JX
Telephone (01733) 898101
Fax (01733) 313524

All Rights Reserved

Copyright Contributors 2001

HB ISBN 0 75432 572 5
SB ISBN 0 75432 573 3

FOREWORD

Although we are a nation of poets we are accused of not reading poetry, or buying poetry books. After many years of listening to the incessant gripes of poetry publishers, I can only assume that the books they publish, in general, are books that most people do not want to read.

Poetry should not be obscure, introverted, and as cryptic as a crossword puzzle: it is the poet's duty to reach out and embrace the world.

The world owes the poet nothing and we should not be expected to dig and delve into a rambling discourse searching for some inner meaning.

The reason we write poetry (and almost all of us do) is because we want to communicate: an ideal; an idea; or a specific feeling. Poetry is as essential in communication, as a letter; a radio; a telephone, and the main criterion for selecting the poems in this anthology is very simple: they communicate.

CONTENTS

Refugee	Joyce Walker	1
The Man With Burnt Hands (Kosovo)	Alison Cameron	2
The Penetration Of War	Marylène Walker	3
A Cry From Kosovo - 1999	Joy Saunders	4
Elegy	Anita Richards	5
The Garden Path	Carol Olson	6
Food For Thought	Diana Daley	7
Little Eyes	Helen Owen	8
The Maths Teacher	Peter Asher	9
The Farmer And His Wife	Ena Page	10
Looking Back	Will Turner	11
Vision	Michael McKay	12
Walls Cannot Hold Us	Fiona Clayton	13
Life	Margaret Marklew	14
Who Lives Down The Lane	Sheila Mack	15
Nature Woman	Jane Evans	16
The Fiddler's Gratitude!	Roy A Millar	18
Man's Dilemma	Jack W Oliver	20
Smoke On The Moon	Roger Mosedale	22
Why?	Lorraine Bridgwater	24
As It Should Be	Frank Shears	26
Little Bird	Pauline Nind	27
Cherished Belongings	Bee Wickens	28
Priorities	Zoltan Dienes	29
The Cross	S P Oldham	30
The Endless Summer	Ann Worrell	31
Feelings Of The Sky	Joanne Wheeler	32
Just Shopping	Terry Daley	33
The Pearl	Ron Bedford	34
Sphere	P R Baker	36
Man	W W Brown	37
A Desperate Escape	Patricia Cunningham	38
The Craft Of The Lead Guitar	Martin Snowdon	40

Choice Domicile	Rosemary Argente	41
Archeon	Helen Marshall	42
Isn't Life Exciting?	W G Whalley	43
Moving House	Derek B Hewertson	44
Cold	Steve Pape	45
Only Me	John Amsden	46
Missing	James Hoxey	47
Ten	Bernard Harry Reay	48
Concrete Jungle	Judy Studd	50
Synthesis	Emmanuel Petrakis	51
It's My Party	Valerie S Brennan	52
Solitaire For Two	Rod Trott	54
Life Is Never Enough	Mark D Kelly	55
The Tune	Emma Buckingham	56
Who's There?	Robert W Shawcroft	57
Dark Whispers	Ria Blackwell	58
The Paper Boat	J W Gilchrist	59
Wet Weather Gear	Ann Beard	60
Remember Letters	Roger Brooks	61
Absence	Elizabeth Read	62
Wrecked	Dave Young	63
Man Murdered Her	Kim Huggens	64
Modern Life	Sandy	66
Streets Of Fear	Janet George	67
Justice	Kenneth Mood	68
Why?	Nicholas Winn	69
A Destroyed Life	Katie Burt	70
Sixteen Little Angels	Ann Grimwood	71
What Do I Do, Clever Dick?	Pauline Edwards	72
Hope's Pathway	Bakewell Burt	73
Unfeeling	J Naylor	74
Independence	Mor Maciver	75
Wanted - A Kind Dad	S Mullinger	76
Why Lord?	Jean C Pease	77
Violent Survivors	Ian Keith Andrew Ferguson	78
Beaten And Broken	Tracy Marie Sheppard	79

Minimum Wage Not Minimum	H G Griffiths	80
Broken Spirit	Ann Hathaway	81
A War-Worn Child	Dawn Parsons	82
The Never-Ending Game	Jean Rosemary Regan	83
Passable Integrity	John Rae Walker	84
Dominance	Reg James	85
Why?	Jean Hendrie	86
Choice	G Bannister	87
Unrest In Ireland	Betty Green	88
The Tale Of War And Want	Pamela Constantine	89
Hands Stained With Blood	Leslie Holgate	90
Ends And Means	Peter Davies	91
Dovetailing	Robert D Shooter	92
Vote For Peace	Archana	93
Redemption Song	Simon P Rossiter	94
Tell Me Why?	Nicky Young	96
Does Crime Pay?	Frances Gibson	97
Love's Solution	Cherry	98
Those They Elect . . .	Dan Pugh	99
Rules	Jean Paisley	100
Cloud Cuckoo Land	Jane Rennie	101
Just Another Victim	John of Croxley	102
Adjust The Earth	Denise Shaw	104
The Cold-Blooded Hound	A Bhambra	105
Mansfield Park	Rodger Moir	106
Family	Sandra Pickering	107
New York New York	Peter Corbett	108
Gladness	A Matheson	110
The Swollen Minds Of Little Men And Women	Alma Montgomery Frank	111
Why?	B Eyre	112
Crazy World	D Riches	113
Conscience	J G Ryder	114
Why?	Lynne M Hope	115
Spirit Of Adventure	Anna-Maria Nicholson	116
A Cry For Peace	Brenda Bartlett	120

From A Child	Dianne Core	121
In Memoriam	E Moss	122
Cyclists	Barbara Fleming	123
With Sympathy	B Busby	124
Troubled Water	S Friede	125
Unneccessary Evil	Lucy Lee	126

REFUGEE

You've walked this road a thousand times
Shoeless.
Warm asphalt beneath your toes,
Footloose.
Played around its bamboo arch
Carefree.
Never dreaming things would change.

Now, you trudge its narrow, winding length
Careworn.
Rain mingling with your tears,
Sadly.
Past on a makeshift cart,
Lonely.
Never dreaming things will change.

Never			Dreaming.

Joyce Walker

THE MAN WITH BURNT HANDS (KOSOVO)

The film
In slow motion, as in a dream,
We watch the men gracefully dance
And hopefully sing . . .
A wedding of life and of joy and gaiety.
Now all are gone - but for one man.
The man with burnt hands.

Beyond the Mountains of the Damned
I search for the man with burnt hands.
One man from Little Krusha's hell.
The only man that remains.

His family's blood extinguished
The fire that saved him.
Massacred by known neighbours
Of long standing.

And now Granny Protush
Gathers the remnants of her tattered family.
Frayed wives, torn daughters,
Fatherless grandsons,
And only one man remains.
The man with burnt hands.

Alison Cameron

THE PENETRATION OF WAR

Clouds further the message
Of tears over mountain
And vale partitioned
Like fields of passion
By bottled bullets and bombs.

Hope a mile long dissolves
Fear and chaos, an order
Of being, no rebellion:
Thoughts like human pebbles
Prepare the oceans for despair.

Marylène Walker

A Cry From Kosovo - 1999

'Oh hear us speak, for speak we must,
Our hearts have swelled with voiceless cries,
We looked to you and gave our trust
And you have fobbed us off with lies.
We need to know your true intent -
Your empty words were never meant.'

The President dismissed our plea
For we were folk of different breeds.
He would not hear! What right had we
As 'Foreigners' to voice our needs?
Our lives, our loves, our hopes, our dreams
Were unimportant to his schemes.

Yet we had spent so many years
Working for all that we possessed.
Would all our efforts end in tears?
Must we, like birds, migrate our nests?
Cast out by ruthless, brutal force -
Is this the plan he does endorse?

We live in fear of tales we've heard
Of villages burnt to the ground
Where rape and murder have occurred
With screams and sobs the daily sound.
Our turn would come! Must we prepare
To flee and leave our treasures there?

Or face destruction to defend
Our rights and homes with hopeless care?
Is it our destiny to spend
A roving future of despair?
While Hobson's choice abandons hope,
Dear God - give us the strength to cope.

Joy Saunders

ELEGY

The only Beings
        at my Wake
will be dogs and cats
birds mice and rats
mallards, hedgehogs and squirrels
and cows and sheep and donkeys
the Tiger if they survive
the Polar Bear and monkeys
and they'd bring their friends
the butterfly held in my hand
the wasp I couldn't kill

But would there be a humankind
to say
'I love her still.'

Anita Richards

THE GARDEN PATH

A picture of Beauty . . .
I chanced upon
one warm and Springlit day . . .
The cobblestone path I walked along,
led a surprising way . . .

Around the bend, were Tulips of red . . .
Lilacs and Hyacinths too . . .
The Jaunty Yellow Daffodils,
sat up in their beds . . .
glancing across at the beds of Blue.

That day when I started
down the Garden path,
In the sunshine, so lovely and bright:
Not expecting to see . . .
Such a breathtaking sight.

I wanted to savour and stay . . .
It quite simply, stole my Heart away . . .

Carol Olson

FOOD FOR THOUGHT

The old tramp was sitting on a seat
Dreaming about what he could eat
He dreamt about some bread and cheese
But the idea of that didn't please
Then he thought of bread and jam
Or perhaps some pickle and a slice of ham
Maybe sardines on some toast
Or a share of Sunday's roast
It could be something in a wok
There again, what about a chop
Fish and chips would be just grand
Or something from the hot-dog stand
Then he awoke with a pain in his head
And suddenly remembered he only had dry bread.

Diana Daley

LITTLE EYES

My love
Has gone away from me.
To a land
I never seen
Where the sky never fades
In the sun
That is sweet,
The tree that is glad
Never cries in the breeze
The flower that's heart is shy
Opens up its little eyes.

Helen Owen

THE MATHS TEACHER

A corridor is geometric possibility
Unquantified potential where mathematically
Lives add to and take away sum totals
                        of the whole -
Chances really do persist where choices
                        divide souls.

Every corridor insists that each
                        unequal heart's
A fraction of its true outcome
                        a random not a part
Of something every corridor exists
                        to prove it so -
That if you follow certain signs
                        you'll work out where to go.

Peter Asher

THE FARMER AND HIS WIFE

Mr and Mrs Brown lived on Willow Farm
They really loved the life they led,
Always getting up early in the morning
And very rarely late to bed.

Mrs Brown would be busy in the kitchen
Baking bread and perhaps an apple pie or two,
She would then prepare Mr Brown's favourite meal
A delicious rabbit stew.

Mr Brown would go off into the fields to work
Harvesting was a busy time of the year,
After work he would go to the village pub,
To enjoy a pint or two of cool beer.

Mrs Brown was friendly with the women from the village
She invited them to her strawberry and cream teas,
They would have a chat about this and that
Afterwards buying their milk, eggs and cheese.

On a Sunday morning the Brown's would go to church
Mostly sitting in the same pew,
Enjoying the sermon and singing the hymns
Later talking to people they knew.

If you should ever walk down the country lane
That runs alongside 'Willow Farm'
You will often meet Mr and Mrs Brown coming back
From their evening stroll - arm in arm.

Ena Page

LOOKING BACK

As hard as we try, for whom that we shall be
and as much as we care, for the one's that we see,
whether it be happiness, sadness and gloom,
without certain prevention, most certain to be doom.
Take hold of yourself and see what you want to see,
be gracious to each other and let bygones always be,
love one another, always be there,
the hand of friendship, a willingness to share.
Leave behind a message, a remembrance of those days
for everyone to look back upon, I'm sure they'll amazed.

Will Turner

VISION

I saw you standing there
like an angel of despair.
I saw you standing there
in the shadow of a closed-down arcade.

We smiled,
closed in and tried to touch,
cold glass,
both laughed and turned away,
just a reflection there,
just a reflection there.

Walk on alone,
light burning in my mind.
One day I'll find
what I've been searching for.

Michael McKay

WALLS CANNOT HOLD US

'Walls cannot hold us' as Jane's friend said.
This is true and in my head
I'm away in the Rhinnogs in Wildest Wales
following Janet Street Porter's traverse through the gales.
She walked from Dungeness to Anglesey's tip
the Welsh wilderness was my favourite bit.

When I was but seventeen I went on a Venture Scout trip
in midwinter to Plynlimon and I was very fit.
It was great, and proud I was to be the only girl
to complete all the hikes through mist in swirls.
But that was then and this is now
standing on mountains like islands - wow!
With views unfolding for miles to see
must be remembered, imagined or seen on TV!

Fiona Clayton

LIFE

How swiftly on the wings of night
Time speeds the hour toward the light.
So quickly race the fleeting years
Through toil and sorrow, smiles and tears.
And where the promises we made,
And all the wondrous plans we laid?
Too soon our youth is gone it seems
And all we own are faded dreams.
Make haste to do, or else regret
You did not reach the goals you set.
No time to idle or delay.
In truth! We only have today.

Margaret Marklew

WHO LIVES DOWN THE LANE

I am the woman who lives down the lane.
Not the little girl of nursery fame.
No child I . . . but a woman of worth.
Now honed by life and given rebirth.
I am the mother of sons.
A person with friends.
With a life I have made.
That, I hope when it ends . . . was . . . really worth the journey.

Though lives, long or short, give us no choice, but to be.
That quality of life is up to us you see.
What we allow . . . condone . . . or share.
Is, up to us.
And . . . life's not fair . . .
Complaining solves nothing and encourages pain.
The days of our life do not come again.
So . . . each day . . . each minute . . . each second . . . must count.
As that's all we get . . . this time around.

Sheila Mack

NATURE WOMAN

At the birth of sunrise
Midsummer shadows, fortean glow
Elysian enchantress;
Casts fertile eyes
Heavenly wings, on
Twilight's incomplete conjecture
Melts, into primeval hot bed.
Concave tangerine dreams
Split, from earth's crust.
Revealed monsters from the ID
Memories last horizon,
Rewrote history
By means of man's premature ejaculations
Chemical flux of bloody streams.
Her stained lips
Have drunk its bitter juice
Her naked belly on ripe apricots has fed.
Danced on Glastonbury Thor
Its pale grey ivory stone,
Uncovered ancient carved dome
A crystal powered gift.
In her amber cat's eyes,
Flashing moons display, Amazon memories.
Purple geographic dialogue,
To angry grey cells, bitter green surprise.
Condense in 'erring' old men's dreams
They're felonious dark majesty
Merging into women's logic with age.
Surrender to relentless
Wailing forest shadows,
Ancestral voices, howling death.
Dreaming of Artemis flowing hair,
Diana in blonde and blue,
Her naked shoulder
Defying construction workers

Assault on green virgins.
Sins of scarlet crime.
A modern day Goddess
Contemplates Felo De Se
Sleep walking, knows she's out of time!
Her lovely face to moon's silver rose
Hidden from society's strange reflections
Somerset talks back.

Jane Evans

THE FIDDLER'S GRATITUDE!
(Dedicated to the six real children who inspired this rhyme)

She's dancing with fairies my sweet autumn child
In that land between night and day she is beguiled
The old fiddler thought of his own favourite verse
She'll dance bow forever sweet Laura's their guest

He packed up his fiddle and rosin and bow
To the Mayfest at Nottamun town he did go
Invited to fiddle down there for the crowd
'I'll give them my best,' he thought out aloud

The fair had a bright sunny day for its start
Rivers of children through stalls all did dart
Candyfloss roundabouts apples and fun
He smiled with true pleasure beneath the hot sun

He played for the dancers some jigs bright and gay
Throw your arms around her and twirl her away
The lads and the lassies retired for a beer
He sat for a breather his heart full of cheer

The air was alive with golden sunrays
His flagon of cider his heart put ablaze
He took up the fiddle and played the gold ring
A tune made by fairies he let the jig sing

A group of small children all gathered round close
Smiling and laughing and tapping their toes
Six bonny faces smiled up at the man
The day became magical how the jig ran

They asked him the questions that all children ask
'How old be that fiddle?' their smiles were no task
Did you make lots of coins in your pockets to put?
And asked if the fair was a joy on to look

The sun was now setting, the day became late
A mother appeared 'We can no longer wait'
Just before parting a little boy said
'Thank you for the verse of the fairies we read'

He watched them depart with a glowing full heart
These yung-uns were charming and then gave a start
They're too young to read yet and realised then
The fairies through them had thanked him again

Midsummer madness invaded his soul
He took up his fiddle and drained his ale bowl
A jiggy quick tune formed up in his mind
In the cool of the evening he let it unwind

The tune he composed is remembered today
A favourite with fiddlers who love this old lay
And this is the story that's still passed aroon
The old fiddler's gratitude is called the tune

Roy A Millar

MAN'S DILEMMA

We know! It's clear!
Don't say again
that science has its limits.
To think this not to be would mean
that man was God;
infinity curtailed
by humble being.

But thought expands,
the boundaries move,
accelerating like the
square of time.

For Gallois,
in his cell,
at twenty-one,
in 1821,
before his death,
by rapier,
didn't know
his pen
would lead
to satellites.
Newton, playing on the beach,
illusioned certainty,
fed man's arrogance;
great appetite.
Only a dream within a dream,
shattered by later mind,
Swiss, Jewish, immigrant.

We have more things,
more artefacts
and refuse clogs the earth.
Homo yes but
Sapiens in doubt.

And now we
face the human clone.
Humility has left.
The couch grass
covers up the path.

Serpents writhe in Eden bright
and offer luscious fruit.
Adam fell the time before
pneumatic mate complied.
He can't go back,
he may not wish, to
Lucy in the Rift
but still he tried to find the track,
return to garden green.

Science seemed the way to go
and then there came the split.
Western world, predominant,
parted mind and matter.
Psyche went its way
and soma yet another.
And science grew
but couldn't teach the human race
to live in harmony.

The silent garden waits.

Is this the way,
the granite path,
cut by logic's lathe
or could it be
that poetry
will take us there again?

Jack W Oliver

SMOKE ON THE MOON

Far misting copse now close appears
In crisp at even snowfall new and
Playing foxes, rusted, bark aloud . . .
Where high and proud and five-a-side
Stark fish bone treetops wave, astride
A long and climbing avenue.

Three trooping brothers trundle in,
Pack and cape, to glade escape from
Blood and more, to damn the war
With all its din . . . bedraggled . . .
Reach the coaching Inn . . .
As winter's chancing sun reclines,
To disembark in lantern-shine.

A coachman speaks of too much snow,
The horses can no further go.
Thus armed with pay and full of mirth,
There, troopers drink to peace on earth.
Their battles won, they rest awhile but
On then . . . over brook and stile . . .
As would all brothers, three abreast,
Across such, push and shove in jest!

Snow-on-snow, deep they go, away the Styx!
With boot-print six, cruel the blow in
Field on field now 'dot' they three . . .
The 'domino' . . . black on white in this night
Seeking out the city bright.
No cannon-fire in drift and spire but
Late, down rutted freezing shire, come . . .
Echoes of Cathedral choir.

Now folding snows shift well aside
For bustling streets all cobbled wide,
Where 'easy women' shout out loud and
Lamplit 'work' a bawdy crowd.
With breath of 'heated kettle-steam',
Thus, stand the three within a dream,
They search out, frosted lash and eye,
A tavern, with no tankard dry . . .and
Not 'too soon' do they espy
A sign which swings a pretty tune . . .
All writ in gold 'Smoke On The Moon'.

Roger Mosedale

WHY?

What had she done
That was so bad?
What did you do
That made her sad?
Why does she cry
Every night?
Why does she cower
And shake with fright?
Why was your tea
Never on time?
Why has she spent
Every single dime?
Why does the housework
Never get done?
Why has the ironing
Only just begun?
Why has your tea
Got too much salt?
Why does she put up
With this assault?
Why does he hit her
Every day?
Why has her life
Turned out this way?
Why are there strangers
Willing to care?
Why would they bother
Especially with her?
Why are they saying
She's better than that?
What do you mean
She's not a doormat?
Why is she starting
To rethink her life?

Why is she saying
No more beaten wife?
Why is she stronger
Than earlier years?
Why is she laughing
And not shedding tears?
Why are her children
Stronger too?
Why?
Because she left you . . .

Lorraine Bridgwater

As It Should Be

Tho thoughts may
Take me far away
And dreams may fade
I still live for the day
That I can recall the memories
Of happy faces
And playful glances
The spring of romances
A stroll thro the park
Then a kiss in the dark
A whispered promise
Of undying love
Yet these were learning days
And we all have a part to play
In the unity of a husband and wife
For the bringing
And beginning of new life

Frank Shears

LITTLE BIRD

A while ago, it seems much more, something precious was given to me
No, not given but lent, I think, for how long I cannot see
A little bird with damaged wings and eyes so full of pain
So broken and forlorn he was, my job, to make him well again.

I held this tiny soul and felt the fear in him
I touched his wings, his broken heart that fluttered in my hands
There will be pain to make you well but trust me please I said
He looked at me, his wounds so raw, with questions in his eyes
Then he laid his head upon my hand, he rested and he sighed.

My little bird is healing now, but it will take some time
He trusts me, he comes to me but still there is some pain
He is so fragile in my hand, I mustn't hold too tight
I must hold him gently for I know he may take flight.

The time may come when he will go, I'll have to set him free
Perhaps he'll stay it's much too soon for him to know, or me
His pain is less, he knows I care, for he has touched my heart
Yet if I had to see him fly, I must feel glad, not sad
For it means he's whole and free, I hope because of me.

My little bird you gave so much although you were in pain
I cannot put you in a cage, I care too much to try
So little bird you have your life, live it as you will
Forget the pain, the frights and fears, let them fade away
You're free my tiny soul, you're free, to fly away or stay.

Pauline Nind

CHERISHED BELONGINGS

I have so many cherished things
With which I would not part;
E'en though they've little value,
They've a place within my heart.
They've lived with me since childhood -
Some sixty years or so,
And I have taken care of them
With the mem'ries they bestow.

There's big Teddy from Chad Valley,
And blue Bonzo without eyes,
One ear hanging strangely,
And a leg that defies ties!
Grandpa won him for me
At the local fairground shy
And, with the cot he made me,
Goes to posterity when I die.

I still have my mini roll-top desk,
Mum bought when I was ten;
It's pigeon holes and little drawer
Still filled, as it was then;
My money box and fancy tins,
And Grandpa's walking stick;
Knife and fork from Dad's war years,
Used in trenches in the thick.

All echoes of a bygone age
When things were treasured more,
And each could tell your stories
Of many years before!

Bee Wickens

PRIORITIES

We have ten minutes before we must leave,
Into this time-slot what more we must weave?
In kitchen sink dirty dishes are glaring
But do we *have* all that *we* must be wearing?

On our return will we gaze at the dishes?
Else wear the clothes against both of our wishes?
I think we should clear the dishes away,
Bacteria ecoli thus well held at bay!

But what strange message wrong clothes can convey?
Your best 'persona' could thus go astray!
Problem of looks, or the bacterial count
Is now the question, the tension will mount!

Let us consider two things: A and B;
What then their relative importance might be?
One might think A's more important than B
T' other B's greater importance would see!

So when two people are living together,
Ranks of importance become a great bother;
Since in such matters there's no rigid scale
Argument there is *of* no avail!

If we slip into a game; win or lose,
We then each other some more will confuse;
If we just *put* our arms *round* one another,
Problems just vanish in such sunny weather!

Zoltan Dienes

THE CROSS

A small keepsake from my father;
A silver cross
Upon a green hill
Of serpentine.

I can hold it in one hand.
It isn't heavy.
The stone is not cold.
It is smooth.

I have fallen asleep with it,
Clutching it tightly.
It's helped me through
My darkest moments yet.

In this electric
Illuminated world,
It's been the only thing
To show me light.

Barely three inches tall
It fills my hand
And fills my world
Orders my thoughts
Calms the storm
And gives me peace.

S P Oldham

THE ENDLESS SUMMER

I thought, I dreamt of this time to come
That I'd find someone so sweet
Like a rose's scent,
- Some sentiment that echoed true
And now here you are like an usher
Welcoming me into the endless summer of love
Before, I never knew or really understood what it meant
Or how happy I could really imagine to be.

I was strayed and easily led
Into danger, so I am still healing my hurt,
Didn't really believe what you said
Found myself looking deeper into your words,
And thinking of you, as an atlas
Whilst all your continents were hard to read
And the meaning was the co-ordinates
Where neither letter or finger met.

Only confusing even more
When autumn never came, no April showers
No heart throbbing of pain.
The forever open door, letting in the only gentle breeze
There was to offer . . .
As I gave into desire
Sweltering with the endless heat
I lazed in your rays
Without a care or mind that bothered,
Because you were there
Whether it night or day
Or any given second of each and every hour
That passed me by,
I didn't notice as you continued to shine.

Ann Worrell

FEELINGS OF THE SKY

She leant forward from her battered window
Reaching from its dirtied frame;
As if to wait in thought beneath the wind
Under the sky with its jewelled rain.

As her sigh billowed out in smoke
Through the still night air,
Unable to crease her thoughts in order
And lost as a shadow, under the moon's heavy stare.

She stared through the darkness for many hours,
Till she herself began to numb like the frame.
And she wondered which rival casted more tears,
Her face or the sky with its jewelled rain.

Joanne Wheeler

JUST SHOPPING

A beautiful blonde lady
Browsing in the high class store
Cool, confident and smiling
I watch to admire her looks
Her figure, her poise and class
Stooping, she tries on some shoes
Stopping, she tries a jacket
But she does not buy a thing
Moving to the jewellery
She tries some glittering rings
Admires bejewelled bracelets
Picks up a diamond necklace
Drops it in her waiting bag
I watch her lovely face
A flush of pink to her cheeks
A deep breath then quick breathing
She calmly walks out the door
I wonder why she did it?
Was it just for the value
Or the adrenaline thrill?

Terry Daley

The Pearl

In the ordinary, obvious alone resides a pearl,
Neglected yet known, in an every day sort of way.
She sits a wonder in the dust and living turmoil,
A pearl of great price, just lying some say, that's nice.
Others just don't notice, pushing just can't focus.
Pursuing image, a great tick in the sky.
To have the great approval, clothed and fed,
Owned it's said, that tick must be an answer.

To me it looked like cancer, a seamy sort of play,
Promising, have a nice day. Payment, oh didn't I say?
The pearl, give me the pearl.
Then there's the golden gates, double rainbow mates.
I don't know how they've got the nerve.
This symbol like big coke, a sort of holy joke.
The promise to Disney-fy the world,
Who after inventing Father Christmas
Took us down an Isthmus, a pincer movement cut us from the pearl
It started with, we have an answer, to we are the answer.
Because we have the tick, we know it's just a trick.
Come buy our consolation, just call it conversation,
Anything you like we're here to save the world.
The comfortable image, but some began to notice,
It was comforting the dead.
Why it's not working, a fool could see.
But they wouldn't ask the question, they trust the tick instead.
One threw a stone customers began to moan, others cried
Anarchists, Some began to tremble.
What of the pearl, the treasure of the soul?
Would it play a roll? Some began to look for new things
That felt strangely familiar.
Cooking, carving, digging a garden, growing shallots,
Throwing the pots, feeling the clay wanting to play.
Breeding some pigeons, growing the crops we get from the shops.

To feed the children with bedtime stories, after filling the streets
With happy games. Curious parents stood at their doors and looked on
Kindly at their little siblings' happy smiles and cries and giggling.
If any sort to control the wiser parents began to howl,
That's not right it's his/her turn, now play in peace.
We've found the pearl.

Ron Bedford

SPHERE

White melts into flamingo fading from a raven sky.
A fox stares out onto darkened meadows, still.
Necklets of silver flare like a chrome bangle, round.
An owl hoots in a quiescent wood.

A natural satellite of semi-precious light
returns to present a dreamy way to the stars.
Brock gazes over a silvery glade bare,
sniffing the cold, wintry night air.

Back to natural incandescence,
glowing bright in swarthy heavens, far.
Shivering mortal souls watch in wonder
as the spectacle dies once more.

P R Baker

MAN

The voice of man is unknown
The power of man is great
The intelligence of man is vast
The love of man is open
The respect of man is acknowledged
The wealth of man is displayed
The fear of man is undisclosed
The saviour of man is a woman.

W W Brown

A Desperate Escape

Wearily, exhausted, over weather-beaten stones she trod,
Wending her bleary way along the deserted route,
Tired, glazed eyes, never leaving the stones,
The beautiful, pale, golden stones of the castle.

Surely she was nearly at her goal?
She had to be, exhaustion was close,
An owl pierced the silence, shattering it to thousands
And thousands of minute, eerie waves,
That chilled their unwilling wader to the bone,
So near and yet so very, very far.

Dark, unwelcome strands of moonlight filtered through
                                        the nearby trees,
Settling on the lonely figure scaling the path.
Her feet ached, her heart was broken and her body was numb.
Proudly like a condemned man
Staring into the barrel of a pointed gun,
She raised her head, amid a veil of uncertainty.
Was she free?

Around her, gnarled branches of wizened oaks and elms,
Reached out to her, calling her, mocking her,
They knew her destination, knew her identity,
They knew how to stop her.

Her shivering bones responded to the searing dampness
                                        descending round her,
Dankness that penetrated her threadbare cloak,
To be accentuated by the whipping wind, lashing her frail body,
Mocking her, goading her into despair.

The man remained hidden.
Why should he help her?

Her only friends, the barrage of stars so very far away,
Guided her over the uneven, dusty, long-forgotten stones.
A path so secret that the few mortals aware of its existence
Had sworn an oath- death would be their reward
If they betrayed that sacred trust.

For her death would be a release,
Not her goal, but the next best option.
Would she ever escape the clutches of her future?
Reach the sanctuary of the faraway hills?

Only one man knew the answer.
Raising his bow, he focused through the rain and aimed.

*Patricia **Cunningham***

THE CRAFT OF THE LEAD GUITAR

You can hear it on the radio,
transmitted from a studio;
but you can't escape the fact it's there,
when it electrifies the air.

No matter what the song may be,
rock, pop, or pure country;
it throbs and vibrates to perfection,
and echoes back in your direction.

The Tremeloes and Shadows alike;
can make this mighty instrument strike;
a magnificent and wonderful sound,
from the walls it will rebound.

No song would be as pleasing,
without its eerie, ghostly teasing.
The crafty way it's being played;
a work of art, that's being relayed.

But, even live up-on a stage,
it's just the thing to soothe a rage.
The lead guitar will set the pace,
and calm the tension in your face.

Martin Snowdon

CHOICE DOMICILE

From Scout Road down the craggy slope
To the horizon, an inverted bowl,
Soundless in semi-panoramic expanse
Smooth, wide, long avenue of trees and grass,
Lonely fires burning within the flanking houses
Oblivious to whatever enduring weather glass.

Shades of green darkened to solo midnight tone
Grazing horses stabled for the night
Bleating ewes quieted by the westered sun
Hikers exhausted, departed before midnight
To consider a repeat performance
Laid bare before the unsuspecting eye.

Her shimmering gown, a terrestrial constellation
Brighter than Blackpool Lights!
Ousting the solo midnight tone
While intriguing salmon-pink sky appears
In place of the sun sublime in all her majesty
This is my town, Bolton!

Rosemary Argente

ARCHEON

Paths lie in ruined solitude,
Grass overgrown the stringent rules.
Willows weep in tears of blood,
Melodic stream now rushes rust.

Green now black and pitch turned grey,
Deep charcoal scars, marks burnt away,
Roundabout cemented, static in its chains,
Disused, abused, the swings decay.

Pit now formed nadir ravine,
Trees swept back to keep filth clean.
Time stopped dead to make scrawled amends.
Gates closed to mark Youth's bitter end.

Helen Marshall

Isn't Life Exciting?

Do you find life exciting?
Perhaps when you receive the post,
You will find you have won some money,
So off you go for a day to the coast,
Perhaps a baby chuckles,
While travelling on your way,
You feel, it's good to be alive,
And you feel like it all day,
You meet a long-lost friend,
Who says 'You haven't changed a bit'
Which bucks you up no end
Life is so very exciting.

W G Whalley

MOVING HOUSE

The sign is up, we're on the move, going to sell the house.
Cover up the bits of damp, hide signs of the mouse.
Stick the paper on the staircase, should have done before,
Been hanging down for three whole years, I tell a lie, it's four.
Pull the cupboards from the walls, clear spiders' webs with mops,
Roll the dust up into bundles, hair grips, pencils, bottle tops.
'That's where it went,' will be the cry, as things return to light,
A tear is shed o'er Tommy's drawing, aged three, of Bonfire Night.
Little Willy's woolly bootee, when he lost it you blamed me.
There's a picture of our Cissy sat out back beneath the tree.
We'll have to stick some paper on the wall behind the bed,
You may say it doesn't matter, been like that since we were wed.
Under stairs and in the attic, all old memories stored away.
Fifty years of pure nostalgia . . . let's stay on till another day.
We'll decorate from top to bottom, brand new carpet in the hall,
Jazz the kitchen and the bathroom when it's done we'll have a ball.
I've forgotten now why we intended selling up and moving on,
It's so big and airy now that the kids have grown and gone.
One back bedroom for a study, the other one, a sewing room,
Change it all from top to bottom, sweep it with a fresh new broom.
Point the outside, fix the roof, and the stack and chimneypot,
Tell you what, I'm feeling knackered, get the sign, we'll sell the lot.
How about a house from Barratt, walk straight in and make a brew,
Garden laid out, beds of flowers, sounds a dream, right,
I'm with you . . .

Derek B Hewertson

COLD

Smiling today, yet still feel sad and dead
I still believe in all the words I've read
The words of wisdom of those long gone
Even these wise people couldn't carry on.

When all hope is gone, I laugh at the sky
I scream and shout, hoping it might cry
Although it could be inside my head
The sky at dawn bleeds a shade of red.

Turn off the lights, what can you hear?
The sound of cars will always leer
Silence like this is a pleasure to me
It helps to come to terms with my apathy.

The stone above my head is heavy and cold
The words that are carved appear to be old
They mean nothing to me because I can't see
I hope they give peace to those above me.

Steve Pape

ONLY ME

I am one
Only one
Out of many
I could be any
Of the lives
That could not survive
Or thrive
On earth
Now no search
Will reveal
Only conceal
What our life
In the strife
Meant at all
Or forestall
Our undoing
Our light too
Creates Creation
Inspires every nation
Man you false ally
Who am I?

John Amsden

MISSING

Gone without trace,
Hammered into confusion it went,
Me, Myself, the true voice of sanity,
The will and self-guidance that sets my secure limits.
Replaced with a grossly intense void,
That has no identity,
Like a revolt of emotions disputing my existence,
It eats further, as I anticipate the climax.

Everything is normal continuing under this pretence,
To which everyone lives under,
Utilising what's on offer in a productive claim,
For the inner peace,
Many people have.

My young, inexperienced voice,
Comes from a place that fights to stay focused,
Amongst confusion and disrespect,
Looking up from the hole I have dug,
I ask may this final plea reach you the way it is meant.

James Hoxey

TEN

Children's voices squeal out loud
Water cascades out from their play
Sun rays strike terror on my freckled skin

I'm chilling again in the broiling heat
Speed cut down from dead slow to stop
As review and resurrection begin

Notes written down on wind-blown paper
Dig, root out all the directions in me
Roads from what, where, when, why and how

Ten years illusions such a long time
Hardly the blink of two searching eyes
The two below my now untroubled brow

Once there was a cruel odyssey
Every twist and turn a nightmare
My soul was committed to employ

But angst returns only fleetingly
To signal my journey's continual growth
She knows I've slowly learned to enjoy

14.5.91. will burn in me forever
Though I'm sometimes obliged to calculate
Our mutual triumph blown up in smoke

But life can be, has to be, re-invented
New roles created from smouldering ashes
Her anecdotes now recounted as jokes

Most P's in my life remain - want them to
Reminders to help keep my frame solid
And so she continues to approve

Maverick black clouds may threaten
But all fail to nail her boy to his cross
Although self-doubt can't be removed

There's a message ringing on the wire
Double celebration is quite fundamental
For two lives in quite different spaces

And while children's voices squeal on
I march to my own, different rhythms
Her boy refuses to merely go to waste

Ten years is both past and present
Storm clouds evaporate to pleasure
Life is how you choose to play your game

Ten years have now come and gone
But her life's legacy surely endures
I'm charged to burn her everlasting flame.

Bernard Harry Reay

CONCRETE JUNGLE

Green plains of Campbell Park stretched far and wide
The music of Global Festival flowed like the tide
A tall bleached beacon beckoned on the hill
Eclipsing Caldecote Lake with white windmill.

Ten silent arcades stretched solitary and bare
We paused at door marked five - this glimpse was rare
To think that earlier on crowds crawled wall to wall
Packed solid like sardines sprawled Middleton Hall.

Fans flocked to Togfest Festival in the rain
Groupies grabbed brollies and anoraks (again!)
Across the road the 'concrete cows' stood still
Rain rasped and hammered houses in Clay Hill.

Stark concrete jungle city built from clay
Roundabouts, H roads, V roads and Redways
A wintry cold summer sun saw prices drop
Arcades burst with bustling crowds who shopped.

Sculpture scooped the landscape grey and stark
Stone grey grotesque figures lined Campbell Park
A bright red neon triangle went pear-shaped
They built a domed new rival called 'X-scape'.

Today the market stalls were quiet and bare
You could almost hear a pin drop (this was rare)
But cluttered spaces spoke of idle dreams
A cacophony of cries and children's screams.

Wild Willen Lake lay south with sailing boats
Grey seagulls soared but moorhens kept afloat
The Peace Pagoda with Buddhist priests
Last but by no means least - the Milton Keynes beast.

Judy Studd

SYNTHESIS

Seeking the truth beyond all the lies
Seeking reality which makes humans wise,
Probing the essence that hides in the form,
The truth that sets free, beyond every 'norm',

Struggling to wake from convention's dull sleep,
Salvaging jewels from the dark ocean deep,
The dust of theologies, the rusting of time,
Polishing the diamond to make it sublime.

Rescuing treasures from monopoly's claws
From a priestly caste, with its rules and its laws,
Fitting the pieces, scattered so wide
O'er so many teachings, distorted, defiled.

Ablaze with the light of life lived and known,
Not somebody's truth, but my very own,
I set all these jewels within the Christ crown,
Then, before the King's throne, I meekly bow down.

Emmanuel Petrakis

IT'S MY PARTY

This was my party
This was the night
The night when everything had to turn out right
We'd waited so long and tried our best
And now all we need were the guests

A new red dress and black suede shoes
this wasn't a night when we'd see the blues
The music was playing, the DJ was great
The food was laid out on plenty of plates

The guests all arrived, there were drinks galore
And then who should burst in through the door
Two special people both dressed to impress
Bullman and Bullboy in black, amber and red

The camera's flashed as I walked on air
Who had arranged for them to be there
I found it was Ashleigh who'd written a letter
She couldn't have done anything better

I opened the parcel that Bullman gave me
And there it was for all to see
A shirt covered in writing signed by all the Bulls' team
This present from Austin was just like a dream

Then a voice shouted 'Mum come onto the stage'
Lisa and Christopher and Claire stood there too,
Saying together 'We've got something for you'
A bouquet of flowers pink, mauve and white
A beautiful bow that tied them just right
Christopher said 'That isn't the finish
Before leaving the stage here's your pint of Guinness

I'm sure I really looked my best
As the Bulls' shirt now covered up my dress
Everyone danced and had plenty to eat
The music and laughter went down a treat

The rest of the evening was perfect and so
By the end I was glowing from my head to my toes
My party was perfect and special as well
What more could I ask on that one certain night
But for family and friends who made it just right

Valerie S Brennan

SOLITAIRE FOR TWO

Solitaire for two
Makes no sense at all
Can't believe we're here again
Back against the wall
Apologise, no way!
It wasn't me that lied
You can keep your common sense
I'll keep my stupid pride

Solitaire for two
Oh what a mess we're in
The deck is stacked the cards are rigged
So we can never win
Apologise, no chance!
Sorry I refuse
You've only got yourself to blame
If you can't bear to lose

Solitaire for two
Is such a lonely game
Some people never seem to learn
And that's a crying shame

Rod Trott

LIFE IS NEVER ENOUGH

Having a friendship
a relationship
going through courtship, hardship.
Life is never enough.
Wanting more
seeing more
having more
not having enough.
Bad times around the corner
good times through the next open door
falling down the trap door of insecurity.
Just existing isn't enough.
The need to feel love
the experience of unrequited love.
To compare the two is enough.
For a lifetime.

Mark D Kelly

THE TUNE

It wanders around my bedroom,
It haunts me when I sleep.
It saddens me more when I'm upset,
It loudens when I weep.
I dream of happy things,
Then suddenly it's there.
My dream is ruined with the tune,
It has become a horrid nightmare.
I look up into the night sky,
A face is in the moon,
A face of a terribly evil old man
On a violin playing 'the tune'.

Emma Buckingham (13)

WHO'S THERE?

It transpires that the Odyssey has gone.
We have been left behind where creation has won.
Jesus is standing on the eternal shore
But we no longer have access - gone is the Odyssey.

Where is the future as we see it?
Is it in concrete buildings, in glass, in brick?
Is the future held in stocks and shares, in monetary loans?
Surely there is more to life than the world economy.

God has gone. He is no longer here.
He has been deposed from His Holy throne.
Where is the God who built the world?
His way is gone, ask any average atheist.

Yet what is lurking round yonder hill?
Is it the sound of falling leaves, on the shadow of a great man?
Why is this tree so gnarled and convoluted?
Is there a hand behind and we see?

Is there a maker of all that we see
Or was it surely man's own exploits?
Was it a stroke of luck, a magician's trick
Or is there a creation behind all we see?

Robert W Shawcroft

DARK WHISPERS

Are you awake?
Can you hear me?
I can't sleep.
I toss and turn in my bed.
No that you will know
As you are just my shadow.

Are you still there?
Today didn't fulfil me.
Nothing feels real to me,
Not any more.

I feel like I am taking your place.
Just a shadow tagging behind.
Lacking character and meaning,
Failing to make myself heard.
I'm not important.
Just a whisper in the night,
That is my time.

Ria Blackwell

THE PAPER BOAT

A discarded news sheet touched by a sprightly breeze
Twisted and twirled in the air, attractive as you please.
This news sheet - once the pathetic blanket of a tramp -
Caught now in the pirouette and flight by a lone street lamp,
Which reflected the swollen gutter full of summer rain,
Its impact on the reader lost, ignored by damp disdain.

But a small boy captured the prize, with wonder in his eyes.

He then folded and fondled and fashioned into shape;
There a newsprint keel was laid to sail out to the Cape.
No battleship or liner was ever built with so much care
To sail the gutter ocean with prevailing winds set fair.
Matchsticks and filter tips and discarded plastic mugs
All help to create a boy's illusion of fussy little tugs.

Pride launched his treasure ship down that crowded pavement slip.

That important gutter voyage was only three feet long,
Assisted through the turmoil by the young boy's song.
Traffic's boom and rattle raise a fearful storm,
Which reminds him of his cosy bed clean and warm.
But all brave sailor captains must stand by their ship,
Especially when built and launched from a pavement slip.

Oh the crying and the pain, to see his efforts swallowed by a drain!

J W Gilchrist

WET WEATHER GEAR

I wonder if it will rain today,
Or will it be sunny and bright?
For my best wellies and brolly,
Will look a funny sight!

Matching wellies, brolly and raincoat,
Is a small child's dream come true.
Now just praying for storm clouds,
Makes all those bad days fun for you!

Wellies of different colours,
Some have writing and faces too.
Made to fit all sizes, which,
Makes your wellies special to you!

Big puddles were made for wellies,
So we can splash around and have fun.
Mud to slide in, making a squidgy mess,
Puddles to wash in, when we're done!

Brollies with decorative flowers on them,
Plain coloured ones, strips and spots.
Clear ones to see where you're going,
Plus watching the snowflakes drop.

As rain trickles down the windowpane,
Plus small rivers form in the street.
So out with the wet weather gear,
Moments of fun one can't beat!

Ann Beard

REMEMBER LETTERS

Thine eyes that sparkle, moisten weep,
All in memory do I keep
The moonlights and a stolen kiss
Heart breaks, memories do I miss.
Would I thou leave this place with me,
But dream of dreams it cannot be.
I wake from dreams to hear clock chime,
Remember here there be no time.

Roger Brooks

ABSENCE

I still see your smile on the face of strangers,
hear your laugh just behind me, and turn,
to be disappointed again.
I follow you round corners a hundred times,
and see you walking through the crowd,
to chase and tap the shoulder of another.
I punctuate the day with my thoughts of you.

I hear you call my name in rooms full of people,
and feel your warmth in bed.
Reaching on waking to touch the space where you should be,
and feel the emptiness you filled just a second's dream ago.

Play our song every day until I'm sick of all the lies she sings,
and hold your picture against my face,
as if you can feel it and know the hurt you've left behind.
I talk to the empty chair across the table,
to be met with silence when I ask you . . .
If we couldn't live without each other, why am I still here?
To carry half a perfect love?
and trace your name in tears on the pillow we once shared?

I watch you grow old only in imagination,
and make up the memories that should be ours.
I will always see your smile on the face of strangers,
I will always hear your laugh just behind me,
and turn every time to be disappointed again,
for the happiness that was almost ours.

Elizabeth Read

WRECKED

Rocks like giant sugar cubes.
A million years formation. An obelisk
of polished slate, and the
waves stampeding through.
Wreck.
Wrecked.
Twisted metal.
Twisted mind.
Charcoal fingers, I brush brave like
across the paper. I make excuses to myself.
Rock pools lost in murky salt water.

Dave Young

MAN MURDERED HER

Where has that time gone,
When Goddess was still alive?
Has the son of man . . . The God of man
Murdered Her?
Tied Her to a wooden stake and set the fire beneath Her feet,
Leaving Her screaming in agony as the flames rise higher?
Have we forgotten Her so completely,
That we destroy Her creation,
That which She birthed in blood and tears,
Each day, to pay for our selfish ways?
We have polluted Her oceans, Her lifeblood,
And stemmed the flow of Her love with dams and diversions.
We have hacked through Her heart with a chain saw,
And violated Her body with desire for land and wealth.
We have choked the breath from Her throat,
Until only the tiniest whisper escapes.
No wonder She hides.
No wonder She shies away from such harsh, neon lights.
Is Goddess dead?
No.
She lives in forests, the mountains,
The rich African earth, and the river sources,
Untouched by man's debased hand.
She hides Herself away somewhere,
Waiting for our eyes to open once more,
The eyes sealed shut with threads of greed, lust, gold . . .
She lives in the thrice-cast circle,
The soothsayer,
The child who, at night, looks up into the sky,
And raises her hand to tickle the Moon.
The one who, when terror courses through the roots of Yggdrasil,
Enfolds her arms around its trunk and heals.

Has Goddess deserted us?
No.
For is not a Mother one who refuses to abandon Her children,
In their time of greatest need?

Kim Huggens

MODERN LIFE

Do you hear me when I call?
Will you catch me when I fall?
Have you time to help in my hour of need?
Do you go where others lead?
Is your life full of surfing and bytes?
Have you looked at the world in plight?
Eyes of people looking forlorn,
Mouths to be fed as another life is born,
Nobody seems to care anymore,
Your life seems like an empty store,
So will you catch me when I fall?
Will you hear me when I call?

Sandy

STREETS OF FEAR

I remember when the streets were free
To wonder anywhere, just you or me.
Times have changed for the worse
It makes me so angry I want to curse.
That murderer lurking somewhere here I know
How the fear burns in our heart and soul.
Walking down the faintly lit street
Our heart is pumping down to our feet
This person does not have the right to rule
Our lives, our homes, our jobs, our schools.
He descends upon our community here
And fills everyone's life with turmoil and fear.
He takes away our instinct to trust
This person has to be stopped, that's a *must*.
We can only hope that maybe one day
We will be able to stroll in our own way.

Janet George

JUSTICE

Violence gets us nowhere,
Peace gets us everywhere,
Faith, hope and charity
Transform our world.
Who needs hate when there is love.

Violence is dark and angry,
Peace brings us freedom,
Too much power is dangerous.
We need to work together to bring harmony.

Kenneth Mood

WHY?

Why must the blood of children spill
And souls of innocents be slain,
Why are they ruled by minds who kill
And blink at suffering, strife and pain,
Why do they seek to rule the weak
And dominate the old and poor
By playing games
With bombs and flames
Under the twisted guise of war?

Why when the starving millions cry
In desperation, want and need
Must politicians yearn to fly
Top secret fighters at high speed:
More wealth and stealth when global health
Could rally with a bit more cash,
Cruel missiles primed,
Well-tuned and timed
To turn their targets into ash.

Why is there hatred on the scale
There is in human hearts today,
Why do so many people fail
To live in peace, and go astray?
What shred of sense in violence
Exists when gentle people die,
The question burns,
But no one learns
Why must we turn to warfare. Why?

Nicholas Winn

A Destroyed Life

Love.
Perfection.
Life.
The importance of this world.
This object's affection.
What we destroyed of this globe.

A smile used to cure the wounds,
The dying lives of this earth.
Now all that people can inflict is sadness.

A flower used to show love,
A plant used to show life.
Now each has become one,
One soul of unhappiness.

This world's individuality.
This place's unique feelings.
They are taken,
They are destroyed,
By pollution.

Everyone has another,
Another one to love.
This world is not a person,
This world cannot be cured.

Now is the time,
Now is the past,
But now will never see our future.
This world's life was taken,
Taken by us.

Katie Burt

SIXTEEN LITTLE ANGELS

Once there were sixteen little angels
All full of happiness and joy
They were perfect little children
These little girls and boys
But one day somebody ended their lives
Without a thought to what he had done
He left in their places, parents who feel empty and numb
People rallied round to see what they could do
But still the reality of what had happened to these children
                                          didn't ring true
What gave this man the right to act as he did?
These were not adults he was shooting
They were only little kids
The only solace we have now is that they have gone to a better place
They won't have to be harmed again, by a person so full of hate
These children will never be forgotten, for in our hearts their memories
                                          will live on
These sixteen little angels that brightened up the lives of everyone.

Ann Grimwood

WHAT DO I DO, CLEVER DICK?

I've got a wife who's frail and old
She had a stroke, her balance went, I'm told
I gave up my job to give her my all
I had benefits then but things went to the wall
The Job Centre sent me a series of letters
'Work nights then you'll care for her better.'
This I feel is just the last straw
They sent me this mail and I'm just appalled
Can't the government have some common sense?
I've had enough and am getting quite tense
Please someone somewhere think of the problem I'm in
I can't smile and I don't know how to grin
Blair has no idea how carers get by
I'm so frustrated I feel I could cry.

Pauline Edwards

Hope's Pathway

Where sadness writes its memoirs
And broken hearts, live our their final days,
Where death; has learnt every word in the dictionary,
And there's no place left in the mirror,
                for the smile of peace's face.

Where the sunlight, rarely shines,
And thunder and lightning have both been stolen,
And now to an explosion's presence,
Alone - do belong.

Where fear, no longer in life,
Has need of its presence to make,
Owning the hours and minutes of each and every day,
- Having become commonplace.

It is here that hope never surrenders,
As saint and saviour, of a way of life,
Which sadly has been taken away,
That those, soon to be born of a new generation,
May see the wrong doings and errors
                of those much olders' mistakes,
And together, may walk the other way,
Where peace has chosen to be their guide,
And to lead them upon hope's pathway.

Bakewell Burt

UNFEELING

They rush in with guns and tanks
Mow people down, all creeds and ranks,
Pillage, loot, whatever they can
Are these wretches born of man?
They take life without a care
Pity for others they do not share,
Women, children they disembowel
These so called men, dirty and foul,
Hack off limbs without a thought
Is this how they have been taught?
Treating humans in this way
A cowardly manner they display,
Villages raised to the ground
People hide, not all are found,
Sorrowful tales they have to tell
Surviving in this living hell,
No more tears can they shed
Starving children, beg to be fed,
Blank eyes stare into space
Not knowing why the human race
Can be so cruel and so vile
Have no feelings all the while,
They terrorise, torture and maim
To them it is only a game,
Why, oh why has man gone mad?
Or has the killing become a fad?
These poor people have not a choice
Someone hear their lonesome voice,
The world must realise and see
These people need you and me,
Help every war to cease
Give mankind eternal peace.

J Naylor

INDEPENDENCE

Heather colours the old matronly hills
In threadbare carpets worn to a dull
Grey scree where the rock spills
Down an impotent slope. A lone herring gull
Wheels timelessly above the loch,
Mourning the passing of the broken-down broch.
A ring of reality in modern mundanity.

Now, fat bloated maggots swarm over the hill
On the wasted carcass of the infamous clearance.
Grouse shooting now where they used to till
And mutton that grazes a people's lost inheritance -
And the blaggart still stands on Ben Bhraggie;
Precursor of that Tory tout Maggie.
When will we free our Land of the grasping Westminster hand?

But that was past and it only gets worse
The clearance is now a quiet decimation:
For now we inherit the nuclear curse
(Mammon protected from defamation.)
Vote *yes, yes* and shout your dissent -
We don't need your Saxon consent
To try and heal the way we feel.

Mor Maciver

WANTED - A KIND DAD

I had thought as a child all fathers must be bad,
But the way we were treated was totally mad.
Beaten for being children, deserved a good whack,
Were average marks at school really worth a smack.
Not surprising that we lack any confidence,
Way we were raised - our cowering natures makes sense.

To dominate all around was my father's aim,
But as I grew older I would not play his game.
Once I stopped crying, he would no longer thrash me,
Now power and control were in my hands you see.
Strange, to other people, he was considerate,
Wish I'd had a kind dad but that was not my fate.

S Mullinger

WHY LORD?

Conversation today contains so many words
And each has its part to play,
But one that has come to the fore nowadays
Is 'Why O Lord, Why?' we all say.
'Why Lord do you let all these accidents happen
And cause so great loss of life?'
'Why when we believe in a God of love,
Why do we have all this trouble and strife?'

'Why are we having such showers of rain?
There's far more than needed to water the grain,
Instead of helping the plants to grow
Our gardens are flooded as the rivers o'erflow.'
'Why are there earthquakes occurring worldwide?
And thousands of people involved have died,
Countless homes have been wrecked by these events,
Many towns lie in rubble, people are living in tents.'
'Why do we get avalanches both of soil and snow?
The ground giving way and falling down below.
Covering people and buildings in their path,
Is there some purpose? Or is it God's wrath?'
'Why, O why Lord, do these things occur?
Is it because thy people do err?'

'Why' comes the question 'When there's a God of love,
Are thy children not saved by the one above?
Please help us God, O help us this day
Get the answer to Why? as to Thee we pray.

Jean C Pease

VIOLENT SURVIVORS

The tragedy of such violence in the home,
By a partner or parent, even in Rome;
Nobody and the authorities do show enough concern,
Until it's too late when pressure does burn.
Some people have the constant need for power,
Wanting domination over the innocent, exterminating a flower,
They are the ones who are forever spoiled,
And are never satisfied until their plan's foiled.
People find others weaker than themselves to bully,
They'll torture them until they're dead and fully;
We can't stop wars that forever surround us,
If everywhere had peace, somebody requires a buzz.
Man is the ultimate killing machine when sane,
At the top of the Earth's food chain;
So when he overpopulates, he maintains the population,
By destroying the weakest people throughout the nation.

Ian Keith Andrew Ferguson

BEATEN AND BROKEN

I woke up this morning with a black eye
I felt no longer the need to cry
It's an ongoing process awaiting its presence
Who's worried about my deep innocence

Why do I not feel I'm to blame
Why do I no longer feel the shame
No longer do tears flow and I wonder why
I keep getting hurt by this cry

The bruises don't hurt anymore
Just the fear of what is in store
Prisoned, too frightened to speak
This is the main reason that I weep

An endangered species about to disappear
Can I stand this another year
Can anyone help me in this sorry state
Or is it to be like this, or is it too late

I await a strong arm of the mighty
Not one that continually beats me
Am I an animal that does a wrong deed
Is that why I sit here and bleed?

Tracy Marie Sheppard

MINIMUM WAGE NOT MINIMUM

I work at a factory for £15 per week
Minimum wage is £3.70 per hour
Because I was born two weeks too early
And brought up by parents with minds of flour

Expecting us to live without
The toys of another kids in the street
Then me being sent to boarding school
For hurting parents who gave no more treats

My other three siblings were taken away
My parents should have joined them too
To be trained to be proper mummies and daddies
To clean the house proper like normal folks do

I ended up at the age of eighteen
In that factory paying pocket money
Hopefully there will soon be
No room for such places in the twenty-first century.

H G Griffiths

BROKEN SPIRIT

Another woman, blesses my husband's arms
This cruel conman bathed with evil charms
I'd caught him, that was my worse mistake
His wrath and fury until evening would wait
Punches rained down, my fingers were crushed
To nearby hospital, I was then rushed
They questioned me, they knew, but I'd not tell
How I lived in fear, that my life was hell
He hid his money down the barrel of a gun
And the baby on way, he didn't want him to come
Often so drunk, he'd punched me away.
I'd started to bleed, I would lose my baby that day.
Drunken words, brawls, violence, shameful blows
But I was married, I'd made my bed, that's how it goes.
We did have a baby, Martin, and when he was one year old
I decreed to divorce him, so everything was sold
They gave me a flat, none of it seemed really fair
For nine months I struggled, then after just one year
He turned up on my doorstep, he'd wanted so to come
To ask my forgiveness, and to see our young son.
I was foolish enough to listen to his drunken cries
We were soon starving, no money, just a family of lies
He'd beat me black and blue, then he'd say I'm sorry.
To this day I can't believe my lack of sense, my utter folly
That a lifetime was trashed, by brutality and abuse
But when you're in love, it's hard to break loose.

Ann Hathaway

A War-Worn Child

Tracts of tears on a dirty face
She looks around this war-torn place
This place that once had been her home
Where she could safely play and roam.

Her doll's remains she finds on the ground
She needs food though none is found
Too young she is to understand
This devastation caused by man.

She sets off slowly down a road
Hoping to find someone she knows
Her home is burning in the dark
Broken trees smoke in the park.

A car she finds and climbs inside
It gives her somewhere safe to hide
She looks out through the broken glass
As men with guns walk slowly past.

Let's pray it's not too cold tonight
Or this child won't see morning light
But on her face they'll find a smile
As sadness ends for a war-torn child.

Dawn Parsons

The Never-Ending Game

It seemed to be a holy war, but as it stands today,
The cause is lost to thuggery, and bigotry the way.
They see their route to heaven, as the one and only one.
Whether Protestant or Catholic, the path they take, the one begun,
Is the one true way, and come what may the race that must be won.

They made their no-go areas, where each sect would take a stand,
And in this way, they ensured a sad divided land.
Many have made peaceful gestures, practised religion as it should be,
But those with vested interests will not let the people free,
Will not give up their violence, or let their people be.

They try to kill each other, and the soldiers we send there;
As they have for generations, in the history we share.
We know the part our ancestors played in this tragic state.
The oppression imposed on them, which sealed the Irish fate.
But why, oh why, cannot a truce be signed before it is too late.

And why, oh why, cannot we begin to live in harmony.
To listen to each other, and let each other's religion be.
For Ireland is a special land, with beauty and promise filled;
And it would be a tragedy if it remained a place of kill or be killed.
So why not make tomorrow the day when peace wishes are fulfilled.

Today I heard of pipe bombs, people injured and maimed.
So once again the music starts, they play their evil game.
Tomorrow they may kneecap a child, or shoot a passer-by,
And once again we find ourselves, asking the question, 'Why?'
How many, in religion's name, will be sacrificed and die.

Jean Rosemary Regan

Passable Integrity

There comes no light before the dawn
In vain the moon hides stars' deceit.
But oh, the glorious river aches
To burst the dam of blackness drear.

Betray no loving, hate each lie,
Discontent in becoming are the words of hope.
If faith, then life, if God then light
For all to see, if being seen.

John Rae Walker

DOMINANCE

On this fair earth bestowed on man
From polar cold to desert air
There is provision for his needs
In countless forms which all may share.

But share he will not always choose
Which breeds contention to o'erpower
By force of might to gain control
And be the master of the hour.

Down through the ages we have seen
Vast mighty empires melt away
'Til naught remains that once had been
And that which was is not today.

And why do opposites endure
Like black and white, like weak and strong,
Is it a fundamental law
Like rich and poor, like old and young?

And do we live in harmony
By will to give and not enforce?
With human nature so diverse
It seems there is no other course.

So halt the violence, my friend,
And go for peace with all your heart
'Twill transcend hardship and bring love
And understanding on your part.

Reg James

Why?

Why do some warmongers,
    Have to invade, their neighbour's land?
Why do bullies, always try,
    To make their victims, obey their command?

Why do some people, have to suffer,
    Their next door neighbours, from hell?
Why can't old folk, get proper nursing care,
    When they're not, keeping well?

Why are some folk, scared now,
    To walk, the streets, at night?
Why do people, of different religions,
    Always, want to fight?

Why can't some youngsters, enjoy themselves,
    Without taking, drugs or drink?
Why don't muggers, and murderers, get longer sentences,
    Cos all those questions, make me think?

Jean Hendrie

CHOICE

The names of the dead
Stretch along the Vietnam Wall,
Recalling those men,
Who are far beyond our earthy recall
While the tomb of the Unknown Soldier
Whose flame, is bright, and tall,
Tells everyone who will listen,
About war, and the folly of it all
Why then, do men choose the darkness
And nations ignore the right.
Why do they delight in killing
And extinguish the divine light?
Man alone is the only creature
Who tortures, and defaces,
In the name of their chosen god
By killing those of other races,
While some nations conquer others
To raise their own flag, so grand,
To justify the subjugation
Of those who really own the conquered land,
In the end, it all comes down to choices
Deciding upon war, or peace,
Governments, nations, and each individual can,
By determination, make all strife to cease,
The very nature of mankind is two-fold
The choice we make, is either wrong, or right,
One road leads to total destruction,
The other towards peace and light.

G Bannister

UNREST IN IRELAND

Violence erupted in Ireland and I wonder why?
Because with the majority they would not comply.
It was never intended we all be alike,
But rather we all a happy medium strike.
They have their faith - we have ours,
We should not try to wield unruly powers.
As it happens I'm an English dame,
For my mother from London came.
But my father had emigrated from Eire,
Long before his marriage to an English maid did transpire.
So I was brought up amidst it all,
And learnt to tolerate it when I was very small.

Betty Green

THE TALE OF WAR AND WANT

How many the souls who live for self alone,
Dwelling in opulent pockets of the West
Nor sparing a thought for the homeless pawns of fate
Or the weary waves of the planet's dispossessed.

How many the rich who dine at smart hotels
Not eating to stay alive but living to eat,
Who gaze outside with surfeit's apathy
Nor notice the beggars starving in the street.

The tale of war and want will never end,
The tide of refugees will never cease,
Till every soul is moved to care and share
And every man becomes a man of peace.

Pamela Constantine

HANDS STAINED WITH BLOOD

Blame not the soldiers for the millions
   of people what have died or suffered, last century,
nor the captains or generals, for they were
   merely the foremen and managers of the politicians.

Blame not the workers who make the weapons
   that have slaughtered those millions,
they are simply servants of their country
   doing what they are told and earning a living.

Blame the politicians! It is they who are directly
   responsible for the deaths of all those millions,
they are the ones with hands stained with blood,
   but remember, it is ourselves who put them there.

We, the people are as much to blame,
   our hands are also stained with blood.
We should think twice before committing our vote,
   bestowing on our politicians the right to commit atrocities.

The millions murdered in the Russian gulag's,
   the millions incinerated in the German camps and the millions
killed in Cambodia and Africa. These atrocities
   were wholly political and politicians hands are blood-stained.

Leslie Holgate

ENDS AND MEANS

Come citizen, don't make a fuss,
Just vote and leave the rest to us,
Land of your birth, land of the free,
For what you get is what you see.

Come citizen, now make your mark,
We'll never keep you in the dark,
With fudge and spin, and Cook and Blair,
The news is truthful, full and fair.

Come citizen, don't make a fuss,
We bombed a depot not a bus,
The flesh is weak but NATO's strong,
Milosevic has got it wrong.

Come citizen, the conflict's o'er,
We fought and won a righteous war,
The lies we told were very small
- Now that's the biggest lie of all!

Peter Davies

DOVETAILING

Adult relationships fully functional throughout
never expecting that,
without meaning to or knowing how
just doing in faith or as the body intended
earth to earth, dust to dust
yet after the thrill of being, functioning
exercising my prerogative
loving mutually procreating like mad

felt programmed for failure, dysfunction
original family dance entangling all
tango performing through all generations
knotted strings throbbing
only steps possible isolation, celibacy
unnecessary parts should be cut, wings furled, flights stopped
yet in reality, or rather in faith, flying high

Robert D Shooter

VOTE FOR PEACE

War is horrible, bloody and sad,
People are killing, people who are bad.
Peace is quiet, calm and nice.

We have many a number just like a dice,
If one of those numbers I may choose,
People may win and people may lose.

Number 6 is a lucky one,
Peace is not far, it's not long,
Peace is never ever wrong.

War is bad, hateful and sad,
I hate war,
But I love peace.

If you love war you must be bad,
Because war is horrible, bloody and sad.
Peace is the one I vote for.

Archana

REDEMPTION SONG

In the highlands of Scotland,
the lowlands of Holland,
the deserts of Kenya
and the forests of China,
people are singing a redemption song.

The song has many different tunes
and many different verses.
People make it up as life
continues on its troubled path.

Now the song is one of joy,
people happy for this life,
thanking God for what he's done
to save us from the grave,
and then it runs
and people start to sing
a solemn wail.

Begging to be freed from life
as prisoners without love.
A scream for justice to be called
against their captor's rotting gold.
Young and old are dying now
for no reason other than
to satisfy another man.

Cannot men and women see
the reasons why our brothers die
to satiate a selfish greed
and act against the flowing tide
of greed and hate
which covers all our world.

Someone somewhere is trying hard
to rescue all our friends and brothers.
Someone somewhere has strength of heart
to carry on the fight for others.
Someone somewhere carries on singing that redemption song.

Simon P Rossiter

TELL ME WHY?

A little child crept into church one day,
Quietly he went to the altar to pray.
'Sweet Jesus, can you tell me why,
You've taken Granny to the bright blue sky?'

Daddy told me she was suffering pain,
But now she's with you she's better again.
If you've made her well, I'm very glad,
But I do miss her, and feel rather sad.

I know you love Granny, I love her too,
She was always telling me stories of you.
Dear Jesus - Daddy's been crying today,
As it was his mummy you took away.

Dear Jesus, please help my daddy to know,
That you are with us wherever we go.
Please tell Granny that I do love her still,
So does Daddy, and we always will.

Oh dearest Jesus both of us love you,
And though you took Granny, you love us too.
One day I know that my daddy and me,
Will see Granny again when we live with thee.

Now sweet Jesus I'd just like to say,
I feel better for talking to you today.
I'll go and tell Daddy that when we are old,
We'll meet you and Granny in your loving fold.

Oh, dear Jesus, I forgot to tell you,
I will love and serve you my whole life through.
Tell Granny I'll try not to cry again,
I know she's happy in your Heavenly plane.

Nicky Young

DOES CRIME PAY?

Child sits terrified in derelict shelter
There's rioting in the street, a car's on fire
Rifle fire someone lies dead in pool of blood
This is Belfast Northern Ireland
Home of saints and scholars
Another home devastated, another child orphaned
Deadly weapon speaks many languages
Black clothes face hidden behind
Horrid mask of evil
'For what crime?' of being Catholic Protestant
'Who's the winner?'
Peace line gradually disappearing
Will there be another atrocity like Omagh bomb?
Drugs, guns immortality where is the day of
Honouring the Sabbath obeying commandments
Race for wealth and mansions of mortar
Where's the justice? Crime pays
Or so it seems.
Neglected children roam the streets
No one at home
parents in the pub
They learn street violence
It's easy to trip an old lady
And take her purse
Crime visibly on the increase
Day by day it's getting worse
Churches, many with closed doors
Because of empty pews
Why Lord why?
We live in perilous times. Why?

Frances Gibson

LOVE'S SOLUTION

Injustice exposes the weevil
Money! The root of all evil

So you wonder why life is the way it is!
Ask, and I'll tell you vis-à-vis
The bee exists to make his honey
But fools exist for love of money

Money makes the world go round
Cheque by cheque, pound for pound
Breathes a death into the soul
Like the pocket with a hole

Money is the friendly foe
Hides the life we'll never know
No imaginations gist
Sees a life without, exist

Like a drug within the blood
Harms us while we're feeling good
Money's instant temporal gain
Slowly builds the spirit's pain

This is where the problem lies
This is why the whole world cries
The fault consists not in our means
But lack of spirit that one weans

Love and money are at odds
Commerce is the fool's false gods
So till money rests in peace
Crime and wars will never cease

Cherry

THOSE THEY ELECT...

Those they elect to Committees -
Who say the way to do things
So that hungers and miseries
Be dumped with forgotten things -
Find semtex and gun
No justice has won
Since time had begun! . . .
But love allied with warm laughter
Mean light hearts ever after!

Dan Pugh

Rules

What fun would any game be without
the rules to play,
yet now, life's rules are being broken
some are thrown away.

They were put there to help us all
to share good things in life,
without our neighbours fighting with
us causing lots of strife.

Man could do much evil unless the
rules prevail,
he can act like an animal who's
been shorn of his tail.

Just like a dog who can be taught
to be nice to us all,
our man was shown how to be great
but, he preferred to fall.

There are lots of good rule books
and God has plenty choice,
he will choose men who keep his rules
and give them voice.

Jean Paisley

CLOUD CUCKOO LAND

Crime can pay, there is no doubt,
As society's do gooders start to shout,
Spare the perpetrator, his youth was sad,
Education, discipline, he never had,
Bull! I say, neither did many,
But they distinguish right from wrong.

Punishment should fit the crime,
We hear of atrocities all the time,
A drunken driver behind the wheel,
Killing another innocent being,
Walks away laughing from the court,
Community service was all he got.

For horrific murder, an eight year stretch,
A little boy killed by a fiendish wretch,
Walking free, no cares at all,
Honest souls must feel appalled,
Total bewilderment at those sat high,
British justice is pie in the sky.

Without deterrent, our crime will rise,
Bullies oblivious to innocent cries.
Judges, juries with heads in the sand,
Make mockery of police teams across the land,
Their painstaking work to catch the beasts,
Rewarded with leniency, beggars belief.

Jane Rennie

JUST ANOTHER VICTIM

A figure draws near to the village She knew
Completely alone now what can She do?
The war came so swiftly some ran - all were killed
While She was gathering food in the hills

Another refugee

She heard the battle it didn't last long
Women and children would not be too strong
Eighty plus now and all cried out
Alone in the world without any doubt

Someone's Mother

Cowering she hides as footsteps draw near
It's only a donkey so nothing to fear
Maybe to ride when unable to walk

All alone

Safe in the hills so they were told
Men gone to battle most won't grow old
She came as bride back long long ago
No thoughts then of war just hard work to show

Memories far away

A family, five children and stories to tell
Life now dissolved into a hell
Then far away a sniper lens scans
Spotting her movements - slowly it pans

Who cares?
A shot and a flame an echoing roar
Slowly her life ebbs onto the floor
Another statistic with no one to care
Dying alone with nobody there

Another local war of little consequence; no one asked why!

John of Croxley

Adjust The Earth

Music plays within my soul
Peace and justice Earth's future goal.
Now we see Earth's darksome night
People in terror, people in fright.

Why is there such carnage in many many lands?
Why does fear and horror reign its way so grand?
Is there an unseen force, a murderer from another world?
That upon mankind in general has all this wickedness hurled?

A general with his unseen troops brought to the Earth great terror
So all mankind do follow him in foolish, absurd error.
Determined in his violent course
To make mankind use might and force.

And in this force he hides the truth of Paradise to come
Where mankind will live full satisfied, ne'er beg for bread and just a
Little crumb
Reports of war there will not be, nor horror ever seen
In this Paradise so great we'll all be king and queen.

Denise Shaw

THE COLD-BLOODED HOUND

He comes out when he is hungry,
He comes out when he is thirsty,
He has only one thing on his mind,
Preying an anyone in his sight.

Silently he comes out,
A mind twisted and
Ready to pounce,
And to catch its prey,
In an act of disgust,
In an act of lust,
As the helpless victim
Lay motionless,
No sign of a cry,
And the last breath is
Almost a sigh,
The cold-blooded hound,
Goes, without a trace.

Grief and shock,
Hurt and the whole world cries,
How can anyone house a hound?
How can anyone but lie.

The police will do their best,
But how can the poor soul ever rest,
Until this cold-blooded hound of a beast
Be put in the
Next best place to Hell,
Would be placed in the cells.

A Bhambra

MANSFIELD PARK

Good sense, like hers
Will always act when really called upon
Names which are thrown in the air
With the person who owns them is gone
Yet she remembers how each of them cared
As she sees her love sail from the prom

This place is so small
There's no books for her to read
Not like her old home at all
For an hour or so she needs
No matter how little or small
Some kind of escape in the reeds

The lovers play you tried to stop
But was never performed in the end
The letters that you posted off
The memory of all your friends

Are you ever to be happily wed
Will the tea things ever arrive
What pretty thoughts now fill your head
As you think of your dear little life
Sat all alone on the edge of your bed
The ever-devoted wife

Miss Price return to Mansfield Park
I shall bring some rod and line
Fishing together until it's dark
Then maybe a bottle of wine
Let Cupid fire that well-known dart
For your heart I intend to make mine.

Rodger Moir

FAMILY

You were not wanted and not fed,
It broke our hearts to see you there,
Not loved, not cared for by anyone,
Only me and your grandfather,
So we sat and talked about the love we shared for you,
And we believed God had answered our prayer,
As me and your grandfather could not have a little boy like you,
So we stepped in and instead of being afraid,
You flourished like life itself.
Your smile so big, so much love you give.
Your love so rare but you show you care,
Even though we found you have difficulties,
Such as ADHD and other things.
We will always be there for our little boy,
As love will see us through,
The hard and good times.

Sandra Pickering

NEW YORK NEW YORK

The two apple halves
Enclosing the whole world;
Butter-stops for ancient love-memories.
Lying, legs up on the hotel wall,
Parted, resting in another time.
This is the bare altar
The Mies-towers sun-washed
In white clouds:
Windmill makers of green pyramid backs.

But it's the angles rounded we need.
The hot-dog congregation
Queuing up for food salvation -
Redemption with tomato relish.
The roads foreplayed
In straight forward canapés;
Visual delights
Leading to bright lights
And dissipation.

The death relapse
By shouting tin-hats
On scaffolds of the invisible hangman,
Stretching skyward
To defy Heaven.
And yet the wax figures melt
Under the midday light:
The raiders of your soul
In boxed glass and concrete homes,
Weighing the Globe
With dollar signs and red wrinkles.

It is too late too soon,
Incubating rare birds of paradise
In adjacent bars;
Prickly pear prima donnas
On billboard boulevards:
Broadway boogies
With seven curves and tinsel.
The drama dream fades
And we are left with signed confessions
Of things left undone.

The square-grids
Pell-mell, running
Hither and thither,
Crossing paths with silk and gold.
The great caveat,
Monoliths of monstrous gleaming folds.
Selling you down the river
Then letting you go
To Hell and back,
Like a blind salmon
Racing back upstream
Against all the odds.
The strange thing is
This is only one part
Of someone else's imagination -
A beatification in stone
For a chosen land.

Peter Corbett

GLADNESS

Gladness glides about my house,
Friendly, courteous, so very nice!
    On the table the glasses
    Are filling with wine
    The plates with food
In the window the mirrors
    Reflect smiling faces
The ritual of taking tea
Is fraught with complexities in Japan.
My friend is speaking of her experience there.
    Words come and go
    Echoes travel in every direction.
    While from the far field
    To the fixed stars silence flows
    To perfect in completion this moment.
Gladness hands me husband
Daughters, sons, friends, a rose.

A Matheson

THE SWOLLEN MINDS OF LITTLE MEN AND WOMEN

Life would be perfect if only the few nasty minded
Men and women would let their neighbours live
In peace and tranquillity

These people's minds swell up to high mountains
In their own imaginations
Watching for every opportunity to better themselves

This happens in all walks of life
In every country in the world
A savage instinct takes over

Once the power of being in a very high position
Life takes on a new lease of life
Anyone who gets in the way is doomed

Innocent people are fed to the wicked
Men and women put in charge of prisons
Persecute the inmates so much they die of beatings

Ordinary people through savage warfare
Turn to wicked ways never dreamed of before
Neighbour fighting neighbour such a sad affair

The peaceful times have gone for ever
Greed has taken over the world
Even the earth tears itself apart, in stricken grief

There are only a modicum of souls that has caused
                              this perpetual sadness
These, swollen-minded little men and women
God, please forgive them.

Alma Montgomery Frank

WHY?

When the perpetrators of violence and abuse are caught.
How come their punishment is derisory, often it's naught
Yet their victims suffer a life sentence of feelings fraught.

We hear of disasters. Floods, earthquakes and such.
Heart-rending cries for aid, our hearts are touched.
Yet corrupt governments and looting mean the needy don't get much.

When will man cease to destroy the earth?
Help to preserve its resources as something of worth.
Yielding great rewards at the planet's rebirth!

Wars and fighting over the whole world abound.
How can lasting peace and harmony be found?
Young people must be taught to love all around.

B Eyre

CRAZY WORLD

God-made this world, he can see
From up above.
When some fool said?
Let's mess it up.
God made the earth;
The skies and the land,
But . . .
Power became the ignorance of man.
God made a world for us all to share.
Then some fool said, for people,
We don't have to care?
God told us all to care for each other,
But now, we start to wonder?
God loves us all, no matter
Who - we are.
But someone had to be better?
Does God see that the world has gone astray?
Still - they mess up this planet,
Still living their crazy way.
If God was you or me,
We would change the world,
As we see days are now strange.

D Riches

CONSCIENCE

As mature adults with reasoning
We live our lives each day.
Responsible for our actions,
In all we do and say.
And if we breed resentment,
As such, indeed it may,
Kill off our sense of conscience
And leads us from The Way.

Thus we gather up our forces
And get ready for the kill.
But to be the slighted quarry
It is a bitter pill.
For the hunter, armed with malice
To do the Devil's will,
Stalk, harass, and worry
Till the prey's exhausted; still:

No thought of mercy, peace, or love
Within the twisted mind.
Revenge eats deep into the brain,
All reason left behind.
And thus, the prey is harried,
Brought down upon its knees.
No mercy for the vanquished,
The Devil heeds no pleas.

Thus innocents are slaughtered.
The guilty have no shame.
The dying prey, soon silent,
Shall shoulder all the blame.
But O responsibility
If conscience does not die,
For we answer for our actions
When we look Him in the eye.

J G Ryder

WHY?

What is war?

To kill and maim
to hurt and lame

that is war

To hurt and scar
to go too far

that is war

To lose a friend
not to pretend

that is war

But what is gained
when men are maimed
when women and children die?

'tis all for greed
no matter the creed
the question is just -

Why?

Lynne M Hope

SPIRIT OF ADVENTURE
*(Dedicated to: - Infamous Castaway - Kingsland and
for the adventurer in all of us - just do it!)*

Oh! Big Adventurer
What stories told
And what you have seen
Reality was - you lived the Dream
Screw one's courage
to the sticking place
that was you.

The lined freckly face
Every line an adventure new,
Those laughing, sparkly eyes
were they Brown or Blue?
Whatever! Your spirit shone through
The Spirit Of Adventure.

Through my life lass,
I've had many stabs in the back you said
But in all I had the last Laugh
The Jungle City was not for me
Sat at a Desk - Technology
When there's a World to see

I want a lion in *my* garden
And maybe more
A friend I told this to,
Why that friend asked?
I don't know why I feel
That *Kingslands* on the map

So Singapore I ventured
Unaware that I'd learn
Of your Big Adventure (in the sky)
In a flea market in Singapore,
Katy told me
'I thought you knew,' she said.
Oh! Katy I had no idea
That Kingsland's not here, but up There.

In Heaven, telling his
tales - Castaway (an Angel said:)
Kingsland I'm jealous stromming
this harp it's been quite boring
but you've lit up the sky.

Yes I felt sad
But a butterfly flew past
'Hey lass,' it whispered
'Tell it the way you tell 'em.
There's not many of us left you know
Not many with the Spirit of Adventure
And you have it girl, never lose it
(The Spirit of Adventure)'

(You once told me)
When a castaway I was to be,
Now look at your picture
In a frame,
Your life was not in vain.
A lion - a tiger
Would tell you.

The face of a lion - but the heart of a deer
Sometimes a little savage
But this was the fear
Of what only the Bottle Knew.
Yet you've seen the luminous
Shining unclouded, sunny
Radiant clear Bright World.

The flowers, the trees
Of every nationality
Clean, Purity.
You've seen the savage Amazon
Zulu King - African Queen
Drums beating
Heard crickets singing
Seen millions of stars
Filling the sky
Life next to Nature
Is like living with God

Oh! Lass they're making
The world dry as bone
Buildings, houses, technology
Making the earth moan.
They're f . . . blind -
Make them see
Excuse my insensitivity.

Somehow,
I hear a song -
'And did those feet
In ancient times
Walk upon England's Mountains green'
The Spirit of Adventure
Still lives on.

There's a little bit
In each and everyone
Live for the Environment
You can't hold
A stone in your heart
Or a technology chip.
But flowers bloom
Forever.

And birds sing
And Butterfly Angel Wings
Whisper silvery songs
And this will go on
If you let it.

Find
Your *Spirit of Adventure*
And take care of it
Kingsland did.

Anna-Maria Nicholson

A Cry For Peace

The sun is shining big and bright
But everything is far from right.
The river is running a dingy red
Sons and fathers already dead
Poppies blowing in the field
Bodies lying where they're killed.

Why oh! Why this bloody war
We cannot take this hurt much more
These men, they don't want to fight
These men who were taught what's right
Governments who always disagree
Do they care about you and me?

Little children never knowing their Dad
Wives carry photos miss what they had
What was this war about and why
Mothers' eyes red from buckets they cry
Religion, politics, I don't understand
Let's live in peace in this wonderful land.

Brenda Bartlett

FROM A CHILD

I am a child.
I was born on the winds of yesterday.
I travel towards the times of tomorrow.
I am innocent and trusting.
And tread the world with an open mind,
Open heart and pure spirit, fed by a pure soul.

I ask you nothing special;
Except what I am entitled to;
Unconditional love, caring, cuddles,
And a warm, clean bed.
I want clothes to keep me warm.
And friends and parents to protect me.
It's not a lot to ask - but I need all these things.

I am just one of the Thousands,
That have never been treated as children should be.

I was born with a God-given right.
I shall die Lonely, Starving and Abused.
But I shall at least know the peace
Of walking into my Heavenly Father's arms.
A peace that I never had
When I was on this earth.

Don't blame me when our Heavenly Father,
Can wait no more for you to put things right.
He has waited too long already.

Dianne Core

IN MEMORIAM

There once was a Doctor from Hyde
Found injecting patients who died
   Over-prescribing pills
   And re-writing wills.
When caught, he lamented
To the Courts he repented
But now he is safely inside.

E Moss

CYCLISTS

We cyclists are a hardy breed
Cycling down the street
Dodging cars and vehicles
Traffic that we meet.
We cycle closely to the kerb
And do not lose our nerve,
Watching out for great big vans
Careful not to swerve.
Some vehicles come close to us
Bringing stress and strife.
We pedal valiantly along
Each fearing for his life.
When the rain comes lashing down,
And wintry winds do blow
We're told it's super exercise
It does one good, you know.
So hats off to all cyclists.
Don't run over one I pray.
Remember if you drive a car
Keep out of their way.

Barbara Fleming

WITH SYMPATHY

Nothing we say,
Can help with your loss,
A loved one was taken,
We pray to the cross.

Help with the pain,
Refill your heart,
A lifetime of memories,
That's where to start.

Our deepest sympathy,
Goes out to you,
With the loss of a loved one,
Someone special we knew.

We feel for your loss,
So bear this in mind,
That someone so special,
Was one of a kind.

B Busby

TROUBLED WATER

Drowning in a sea of self pity
Third time down and losing control
Troubled water everywhere
Must build a *bridge* to settle my soul.

I need a *rock* - an island of dreams
A gentle *Cecilia* to realise my schemes . . .

. . . A *satisfied customer* in a room full of friends;
Achieving my goal before the *book ends!*

S Friede

UNNECESSARY EVIL

Why is everything changing?
What use is all this killing?
Why can't people live together?
Some would murder for a shilling
What's happened to loyalty?
Some people's got a heart of stone
What good is rushing through life
You'll only end up alone.
I never saw the sense
Of the 1st and 2nd World Wars
Why everyone had to be in the dark
In their homes behind closed doors.
Men and women gave their lives
So the World could all be free
But still the wars go on
It doesn't make sense to me.
What makes some people that way?
Believe me I don't know why
But still some get away with it
They steal, they cheat, they lie,
But there is some beauty in this world
It's waiting for us somewhere
It's there for those who want it
Waiting for us all to share
But some people are born angry
I can't fathom it out
They still think it's something
To brag and boast about
'Stop hating' let all the bad things cease
So all of us can live in peace.

Lucy Lee

SUBMISSIONS INVITED
SOMETHING FOR EVERYONE

POETRY NOW 2001 - Any subject, any style, any time.

WOMENSWORDS 2001 - Strictly women, have your say the female way!

STRONGWORDS 2001 - Warning! Age restriction, must be between 16-24, opinionated and have strong views. (Not for the faint-hearted)

All poems no longer than 30 lines. Always welcome! No fee! Cash Prizes to be won!

Mark your envelope (eg *Poetry Now) 2001*
Send to:
Forward Press Ltd
Remus House, Coltsfoot Drive,
Peterborough, PE2 9JX

OVER £10,000 POETRY PRIZES TO BE WON!

Judging will take place in October 2001